THE LITTLE BOOK OF
PARIS

Published in 2022 by OH!
An Imprint of Welbeck Non-Fiction Limited,
part of Welbeck Publishing Group.
Based in London and Sydney.
www.welbeckpublishing.com

Compilation text © Welbeck Non-Fiction Limited 2022
Design © Welbeck Non-Fiction Limited 2022

Disclaimer:

ISBN 978-1-80069-025-7

Compiled and written by: Mathilde Pineau-Valencienne
Editorial: Vicroria Godden
Project manager: Russell Porter
Design: Tony Seddon
Production: Arlene Alexander

A CIP catalogue record for this book is available from the British Library

Printed in China

10 9 8 7 6 5 4 3 2 1

Illustrations: Freepik.com

THE LITTLE BOOK OF

PARIS

THE ROMANCE CAPITAL
OF THE WORLD

CONTENTS

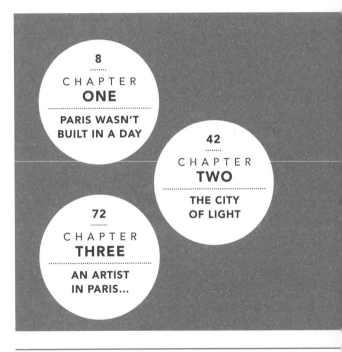

PARIS, THE WORLD'S MOST ICONIC CITY

Paris has long been one of the top three most visited cities in the world, attracting a record-breaking 38 million visitors in 2019. Also known as the "City of Love" and the "City of Light", it is the home to iconic landmarks and museums such as the Sacré-Coeur, the Eiffel Tower, the Louvre, and more recently the Atelier des Lumières (Studio of Lights), as well as world-famous restaurants and *haute couture* brands.

Behind the shimmering glamour of this iconic metropolis, however, Parisians are used to a lot of "merde". They'll tell you it's expensive, overcrowded, polluted and full of tourists. That the streets are littered with dog poo and cigarette butts, there are nasty smells on the Métro (when there isn't a strike), sky-high rent and house prices, not to mention the exorbitant cost of a coffee when all you need is a break to enjoy the view.

Despite all this, Paris remains a dream city for most citizens of the world. Its beauty and charm mixed with its raw and rugged character give it a fascinating, awe-inspiring mystery.

The city's architecture has been extremely well preserved, even during World War Two. In recent years, regeneration of peripheral areas into residential neighbourhoods and new business districts such as "La Défense" and "Station F" (the centre of French tech) have brought a modern look and vibe to Paris, with better transport connections to Greater Paris, "la banlieue".

This book is for Paris lovers, but also for those who have yet to visit or those desperate to return.

Paris wasn't built in a day

The history of Paris is marked with much violence and beauty, and can be described as the epicentre of France's three all-consuming passions: politics, art and love.

Thanks to the quality of its preservation through the ages, the whole city is like an outdoor walkable museum.

66

What an immense
impression Paris made
upon me. It is the most
extraordinary place in
the world!

99

Charles Dickens

The Roman name of
the city was *Lutetia*,
which meant "swamp"
or "marsh" in Gaulish
and "dirt" or "mud' in
Pro-Celtic. Yes, the City
of Light was initially
a large pile of mud.

The exact location of the original settlement of Paris is still a mystery.

Historians have debated that it lies in Ile de la Cité, but it was proven by other historians that the first settlers were farming in the Louvre location, and even earlier at Nanterre, much further west.

The Seine river used to
run in a zigzag, which
flooded on regular
occasions, hence the
"swamp" appellation
of *Lutetia*.

Paris is still ruled by the Seine's flooding. Approximately once every hundred years, the Seine tends to overflow and revert to its old course. During the Great Flood of 1910, train stations such as Gare de Lyon and Gare Saint-Lazare were completely underwater!

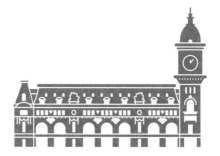

Fluctuat nec mergitur.

([She] is rocked [by the waves], but does not sink)

Latin motto of the city of Paris

Paris until the 19th century was one of the largest ports of France. Its coat of arms features the shape of a boat.

The Zouave, a statue sited on the Pont de l'Alma, is used as an informal flood marker for the level of the River Seine in Paris.

The Romans conquered the Gauls in 52 BC, and there are still beautiful remains of the Roman era, such as the Lutetia arena. It was found by complete coincidence in 1869, when building work began on a warehouse for omnibuses on rue Monge (5th arrondissement), much to the surprise of historians, who had been trying to locate it for years.

It is a hidden gem in Paris few tourists know about, tucked in on the side of the street where you can sit down, have a picnic, and lose yourself in the ages of time.

Other remains that were found by accident were of the medieval fortress of the Louvre Palace, which was then called the Palais de Saint-Paul.

The plinth of the donjon and its ditch were uncovered in 1983 when the square courtyard of the Louvre Palace was being excavated for the construction of the glass pyramid.

In Paris, monarchs have had, over the centuries, five official residences: the Palais de la Cité (now called Palais de la Justice), the Palais de Saint-Paul, the Louvre, the château de Vincennes and the Tuileries.

66

England has built
London for its own use.
France has built Paris for
the entire world.

99

Ralph Waldo Emerson

Since the Middle Ages, Paris has been a centre for university education.

The most famous college, the Sorbonne, was created in 1257. The students spoke Latin, resulting in the christening of Saint Geneviève's Mount as the Latin Quarter.

"

I never rebel so much against
France as not to regard Paris
with a friendly eye; she has had
my heart since my childhood…
I love her tenderly, even to her
warts and her spots. I am French
only by this great city: the glory
of France, and one of the noblest
ornaments of the world.

"

Michel de Montaigne

It took more than 150 years to build Notre-Dame Cathedral. It is an exceptional 127 metres long and its gothic style is one of the most beautiful in Europe.

In the early 19th century, Notre-Dame was so derelict that it was nearly torn down.

It was Victor Hugo who saved the day with *The Hunchback of Notre-Dame*. Thanks to his novel, Parisians became aware of the situation and campaigned for its preservation.

66

Is Paris burning?

99

**Adolf Hitler's question to his chief
of staff Alfred Jodl on the eve of the liberation
of Paris in 1944**

66

Even the darkest
night will end and
the sun will rise.

99

Victor Hugo, *Les Miserables*, 1862

24–29 August 1572
were among the deadliest
nights of Paris' history, with
several thousand Protestant
leaders massacred by surprise
after attending the wedding
ceremony of Marguerite
de Valois and the future
King Henry IV.

After 30 years of civil war, Henry IV's return to Paris marked the end of the religious divide between the Catholics and the Protestants.

The oldest tree in Paris
is a black locust planted
in square Viviani
(5th arrondissement)
in 1602.

The oldest bridge in Paris is ironically called the New Bridge, "le Pont Neuf".

It is also the longest (238m) in the city and was built by Henry IV in 1607.

"

To study in Paris is to be born in Paris!

"

Victor Hugo, *Les Misérables*, 1862

As the 17th century rolled on, Paris became an open, more extensive city, lit by around 2,700 candle lanterns, which gave birth to its nickname of "the City of Light", or *la Ville-Lumière*.

Paris' most beautiful view from the Louvre, the Tuileries, up to the Arc de Triomphe, was the vision of Louis XIV. One of the most famous avenues in the world, the Avenue des Champs Élysées was a demonstration of the Sun King's monumental power.

66

Ah, if I were not king, I should lose my temper.

99

Louis XIV

66

Dare to think for yourself.

99

Voltaire

In the 18th century Paris became the intellectual centre of Europe with philosophers and writers such as Voltaire, Montesquieu, Jean-Jacques Rousseau and Benjamin Franklin calling the city home.

At the top of the Bastille column, built on the site of the famous prison, which was demolished on 14 July 1789 during the French Revolution, shines the golden statue of the Spirit of Freedom.

The city of Paris offered a diamond necklace as an engagement present to Empress Eugénie, future bride of Napoleon III.

She refused it and asked for its sale to fund a house for orphans, the building for which still exists today. The architect designed it in the form of a diamond necklace!

(Doesn't this true story beat the diamond story in the film *Titanic*?)

Known as one of the most beautiful brasseries in Paris, Le Bofinger is a culinary institution of the city.

Located between Place de la Bastille and Place des Vosges, it is known for serving the best sauerkraut cooked in the traditional way.

Paris is one of the
top three most visited
cities in the world,
attracting close to
40 million visitors
each year.

CHAPTER
TWO

The City of Light

Paris' landmarks are world-renowned symbols of architectural beauty: the Eiffel Tower, the Arc de Triomphe, Notre-Dame Cathedral… few cities in the world have more recognizable landmarks than Paris.

Although the nickname "The City of Light" originated from the fact that Louis XIV made the city more secure with lantern-lit streets, it also resonates with the Age of Enlightenment, when Paris was the hub of democratic ideas as well as, nowadays, the stunning lighting of the city illuminated like a stage.

Paris' top 10 most visited cultural venues

The Sacré-Coeur

The Louvre

The Eiffel Tower

The Pompidou Centre

The Musée d'Orsay

The National Natural History Museum

The City of Science and Industry

The Arc de Triomphe

The Sainte-Chapelle

Atelier des Lumières (Studio of Lights)

66

There are only two
places in the world where
we can live happy: at
home and in Paris.

99

Ernest Hemingway

The Eiffel Tower is one of the most iconic monuments in the world. It embodies the French spirit, *grandeur*, style and mood.

After the events of the Paris attacks in 2015, its 20,000 sparkling lights went dark as a sign of national mourning.

When the French became the world football champions in 2018, the blue, white and red colours of the French flag clad the Iron Lady to celebrate the return of their heroes.

Since 1 January 2000, the Eiffel Tower shines with shimmering lights at night time, every hour, on the hour, for five minutes until 1 a.m.

In addition, the beacon on the summit successively sweeps a quarter of the horizon on a rotation system, which gives the illusion of a turning light.

66

A thousand times have
I wished for the Eiffel
Tower to find itself at the
bottom of the river.

99

Julien Green

When Paris was freshly freed from the Nazis in 1945, the first floor of the Eiffel Tower became a nightclub reserved for American GIs.

Jean Julien's *Peace for Paris* illustration became a symbol of solidarity with the victims of the Paris attacks in November 2015. It was relayed as a profile image by millions of social-media users around the world, along with the phrase "Je suis Paris".

On 15 April 2019, the world looked on in horror and disbelief as a fire engulfed the roof of Notre-Dame and the 800-year-old spire collapsed.

The cathedral is due to be fully restored by 2024, when Paris will host the Olympic Games.

On the spot of the Basilica of the Sacré-Coeur, at the start of the 3rd century, the first Christians of Paris, with their bishop Saint Denis, were martyred, giving the hill its name, Montmartre, which means "Mount of Martyrs".

"

To breathe Paris is to preserve one's soul.

"

Victor Hugo, *Les Misérables*, 1862

In 2019, 11 million visitors entered the Basilica of the Sacré-Coeur at the top of the hill of Montmartre.

This monument is highly distinctive in the Parisian skyline as it's located on the highest point of the hill. Its gleaming white colour and Romano-Byzantine architectural style were inspired by the Hagia Sofia in Istanbul and St Mark's Basilica in Venice.

You must climb 270 steps to discover one of the most beautiful views of Paris.

During the Revolution, the
Place du Carrousel at the Louvre
was renamed "Place de la Fraternité"
(Fraternity Square), and a guillotine
was temporarily placed there.

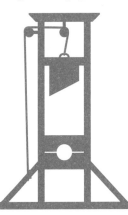

Top 10 free things to do in Paris

The open-air cinema in the
Parc de la Villette (during July and August)

The Jardin du Luxembourg

The Sacré-Coeur and the Wall of Love
around the corner

Notre-Dame Cathedral

The Père Lachaise cemetery

Atelier Brancusi

La Promenade Plantée

A late-night picnic at the
Square du Vert-Galant

A fashion show at Galeries Lafayette

With its 440,000 square metres, the Père Lachaise cemetery feels like a city within the city. It is the most visited cemetery in the world with an impressive A-list of tomb owners.

One of its most famous grandiose tombstones is that of Oscar Wilde. The tradition is to kiss it with red lipstick for good luck in love.

❝

Lunch kills half of Paris, supper the other half.

❞

Charles de Montesquieu

La Tour d'Argent, one of
Paris' most renowned
restaurants, first opened in
1582 at 15 quai de la Tournelle.

La Marquise de Sévigné, a
literary star of the late
17th century, famously drank
liquid chocolat there for
the first time.

The Louvre Museum hosts one of the most prestigious art collections of the world.

You will find Delacroix's masterpiece *Liberty Leading the People*, which symbolizes the spirit of revolution, for which Paris is the main stage.

The City of Love has lost its love-locks bridge (Pont des Arts) forever!

The 1 million locks weighed over 45 tons and had to be removed to prevent structural damage. The bridge has been redecorated with modern, art-deco designs.

"

Paris is always a good idea.

"

Audrey Hepburn in the movie *Sabrina*, 1954

As we all know, Bastille Day is celebrated each year on 14 July to commemorate the invasion of the Bastille prison by the people of Paris in 1789. The most famous prisoner at the time was the Marquis de Sade. Ironically, he had managed to be evacuated to a nicer prison only one week before the Revolution!

Today, in the centre of the Bastille square resides the famous *Génie de la Liberté* (Spirit of Freedom) at the top of the column to commemorate the Revolution of 1830. In *Les Misérables*, Victor Hugo had set the home of Gavroche under an elephant sculpture, which had been initially built to decorate the Bastille Square.

Today *Eau de Paris* provides exceptionally high-quality, free, drinkable water from 190 water points available on streets of the city and a further 335 in parks and green spaces.

River banks are now car-free
between Bastille Square
and the Eiffel Tower, 2.3km
on the left bank and 3.3km on
the right bank. With green
spaces, bars and restaurants,
picnic zones, sports equipment
and zen areas, it's the spirit of
"Paris Plages", the temporary
beach set up for the summer,
but all year long!

In 2018, there were 2,348 cultural venues in Paris and Greater Paris.

66

To understand Paris, you must sit in a café – perhaps at a sidewalk table beneath lush plane trees facing a broad boulevard or historic square, perhaps on a leatherette banquette inside a dim neighborhood bar/tabac on an obscure side street. You must sip an espresso, a Perrier, a glass of wine, whatever, and watch the world go by.

Angela Mason

"

In Paris, our lives are one masked ball.

"

Gaston Leroux, *The Phantom of the Opera*, 1909

Underground Paris welcomes you with 6 million skulls in the Catacombs. From Place Denfert-Rochereau, if you descend the 131 steps, you will walk through walls of skulls and bones for 1.7km, where famous literary and political figures such as La Fontaine, Rabelais, Robespierre, Charles Perrault, Fouquet, Colbert and Rameau lie unidentified. They were exported from cemeteries in the town centre to the quarries of the Tombe-Issoire. A unique visitor experience if ever there was one!

Paris' 2021 population is now estimated at more than 11 million.

The Champs Elysées, literally "the paradise of Greek gods", where the Arc de Triomphe lies, was built to celebrate the Sun King, Louis XIV. It is the epicentre of Paris' glory.

The French national football team famously descended upon the avenue twice, in 1998 and 2018, to celebrate their World Cup win.

CHAPTER
THREE

An Artist in Paris…

Throughout the ages, Paris has always been a cultural hub, known as the ultimate destination for artists in search of inspiration.

Van Gogh lived in Paris for a few years, as did Cézanne, Monet, Manet, Renoir, Modigliani, Picasso… The end of the 19th century and the beginning of the 20th was truly a golden era for the city.

An artist has no home in Europe except in Paris.

Nietzsche

Cabarets were the ancestors of cafés, where artists and writers liked to meet and dine out.

La Fontaine, Molière and Racine were known for being regulars at the Mouton Blanc cabaret, rue du Vieux-Colombier (in the 6th arrondissement).

Theatres have been at the heart of Parisian culture since the 17th century.

In 1641, Le Grand Théatre de Richelieu (now called La Comédie Française) at the Palais Royal could host 1,200 spectators. It was here that Molière suffered a fatal on-stage collapse while playing *Le Malade Imaginaire*.

66

My Paris is a land where twilight days

Merge into violent nights of black and gold

99

Arthur Symons

In 1784, the premiere of the subversive play *Le Mariage de Figaro* was a great success. 4,000–5,000 people tried to get in to what was one of the most significant events in the history of French theatre.

66

The Moulin Rouge. A night club, a dance hall and a bordello [...] A kingdom of night time pleasures. Where the rich and powerful came to play with the young and beautiful creatures of the underworld.

99

Moulin Rouge, 2001

"

Paris was a museum displaying exactly itself.

"

Jeffrey Eugenides

The Louvre as a museum was created after the Revolution in 1793.

The *Mona Lisa* first came on display in 1796; the entrance was free but the dress code was still smart!

The 10 best places to view art

Dalì Paris

Passage Verdeau

Le cent Quatre

Cartier Foundation

Le Marché de la Création de
Paris Montparnasse

Ateliers-musée Chana Orloff

Galerie Sakura

Galerie de Medicis

Artcurial

Galerie Bartoux

66

In Paris, everybody
wants to be an actor;
nobody is content to
be a spectator.

99

Jean Cocteau

"

Usually, the murmur that rises up
from Paris by day is the city talking; in
the night it is the city breathing; but here
it is the city singing. Listen, then, to this
chorus of bell-towers – diffuse over the
whole murmur of half a million people
– the eternal lament of the river – the
endless sighing of the wind – the grave
and distant quartet of the four forests
placed upon the hills, in the distance,
like immense organ pipes – extinguish
to a half light all in the central chime
that would otherwise be too harsh
or too shrill;

and then say whether you know of anything in the world more rich, more joyous, more golden, more dazzling, than this tumult of bells and chimes – this furnace of music – these thousands of brazen voices, all singing together in flutes of stone three hundred feet high, than this city which is but one orchestra – this symphony which roars like a tempest.

Victor Hugo, *The Hunchback of Notre-Dame*, 1831

"Electro: From Kraftwerk to Daft Punk", at the Philharmonie de Paris, was the world's largest exhibition about electronic music to date. It took place in 2019 and travelled to London in 2020.

The chief danger
about Paris is that
it is such a strong
stimulant.

T.S. Eliot

Intellectual Parisian life is characterized by its café culture.

The oldest and most famous, frequented by Voltaire, Jean-Jacques Rousseau and Benjamin Franklin, is the lavishly decorated Café Procope, which opened in 1686 at the heart of Saint-Germain des Prés in the 6th arrondissement .

In Saint-Germain des Prés,
the café Les Deux Magots
was the headquarters of
Jean-Paul Sartre and Simone
de Beauvoir.

Sartre famously collected the
clients' leftover cigarette butts
to stuff his pipe.

66

The best of America drifts to Paris. The American in Paris is the best American.

99

F. Scott Fitzgerald

Impressionists in the late
19th century favoured the
Café Guerbois in Montmartre.
Édouard Manet, Claude Monet,
Camille Pissarro and Émile Zola
were all regulars.

The cabaret Le Chat Noir
was also renowned for attracting
artists of the time and hosting
the first shadow theatre in Paris.

In *A Moveable Feast*, Ernest Hemingway tells about his daily Parisian life in the early 1920s. In those days, you could fish in the Seine and buy fresh goat's milk from goat herders in the street.

After the First World War
Pablo Picasso, Georges Braque and
Fernand Léger famously gathered
at the Brasserie La Closerie des
Lilas in Montparnasse, where
artists' residencies were developing,
such as *La Ruche* (*The Beehive*).

"

Under the Mirabeau Bridge
there flows the Seine

Must I recall

Our loves recall how then

After each sorrow joy came
back again.

"

Guillaume Apollinaire

Since 1891, the *bouquinistes* have set up their bookstalls along the left bank of the Seine, between the Arab World Institute (IMA) and the University of Fine Arts (Les Beaux Arts). There are 240 in total and their book box can be a maximum of 2 metres long, 0.75 metres wide and 2.1 metres high when open.

"

I created this bookstore like
a man would write a novel,
building each room like a chapter,
and I like people to open the door
the way they open a book, a book
that leads into a magic world in
their imaginations.

"

George Whitman about the independent bookstore
Shakespeare and Co.

Since 1669, the Opéra de Paris
changed location 15 times until
1875, when the Palais Garnier
was finally completed and
inaugurated after 15 years
of building work.

Its architectural style was
highly criticized at the time,
just like its contemporary twin,
the Opéra de Bastille, which
opened in 1989.

"

These are hard times for dreamers.

"

Amélie, 2001

The Louvre is the world's largest art gallery and museum. It has over 38,000 pieces of art within its walls. It is also the most visited art gallery on the planet!

In May 1968, the Odéon Theatre was occupied by students from the Latin Quarter. They took ownership of the building and held political assemblies in the majestic centre stage.

The famous Bloody Mary cocktail was invented in Paris at the Ritz Hotel. Legend says that this popular tipple was made for Ernest Hemingway when he requested a drink that didn't smell like alcohol!

66

America is my country and Paris is my hometown.

99

Gertrude Stein

In 2005, Tom Cruise asked
to become an honorary citizen
of the city of Paris, but the
town hall put a block on it
because of his affiliation
with Scientology.

The largest rooftop of Paris is at the top of L'Arche de la Défense, the contemporary twin to the Arc de Triomphe. Inaugurated on 14 July 1989 for the bicentenary of the French Revolution, it offers a terrace of 1,000 square metres with a 360-degree view of Paris.

66

never
even in calmer times
have I ever
dreamed of
bicycling through that
city
wearing a
beret

99

Charles Bukowski, "Paris"

CHAPTER
FOUR

From *Paname*, with Love

Paname is a common nickname for Paris.

The city life would not be vibrant without its neighbourhoods/quartiers (Saint Germain, Montmartre, Le Marais…), where Parisians shop at farmers' markets, sit at café terraces for hours on end, or sip an apéritif while enjoying the view onto the squares or Paris rooftops.

66

I was born in Paris, and have
spent my whole life here.
I'm basically the ultimate Parisian.
There's so much to do and I can't
imagine living anywhere else.
Maybe one day, when I'm older, I'll
want to leave. But right now,
I just want to be here, living life,
and hanging out in café terraces.

99

Tristan Lopin (French stand-up comedian)

Paris intra muros (Paris within the walls) has 2.19 million inhabitants and Greater Paris, the banlieue, 6.81 million.

The Périphérique, the multi-lane ring-road around Paris, marks the frontier of the city with the banlieue.

La Palette in the 6th arrondissement is a vintage café famous for its artist regulars throughout the century – Picasso of course, and Harrison Ford today! It's been repeatedly hailed as the best outdoor café in Paris.

La Maison Rose, on the corner of rue de l'Abreuvoir and rue des Saules in Montmartre, has been serving up coffee for over 100 years.

It was painted in pink and remodelled in 1920 by the owner Laure Germaine, who was once the muse and lover of Picasso. Now more of a hip destination, it was once an artist haven!

Iconic retro signatures of Paris date back to the end of the 19th century and early 20th: look out for the charming carousels in the parks, the wooden swings, miniature sailboats at the Jardins du Luxembourg or the Tuileries, the Art Nouveau style of the first generation of Métro entrances, and the dark green newspaper and advertising kiosks (les colonnes Morris).

❝

The terrifying
and edible beauty
of Art Nouveau
architecture.

❞

Salvador Dalì

Paname is the colloquial name for Paris and its suburbs. It captures the authentic spirit of the Parisian working class but, as Paris gets more and more expensive, it has become less applicable.

However, it's still used, as the movie *Amélie* demonstrated so charmingly in its portrait of everyday life in Montmartre.

Why are Paris' arrondissements (boroughs) shaped like a snail shell?

In 1870, Paris appended neighbouring villages such as Montmartre and Montparnasse. The number of boroughs grew from 12 to 20 but the 13th was going to fall under the chic West of Paris. So, the mayor of the western boroughs managed to convince the prefect, Georges-Eugène Haussmann, to change the numbering from left to right, top to bottom, to a spiral from the city centre to its outskirts. Money – and superstition – talks!

"

I love Paris when it sizzles.

"

The Cole Porter song, which was used as a title for a film with Audrey Hepburn

It's midnight. One half of Paris is making love to the other half.

Ninotchka, 1939

There is no guillotine left in Paris… but you will find five concrete spots where a former guillotine was located, at the corner of Roquette and La Croix-Faubin street. They're in front of what was once a prison. The old guillotine was concreted there in 1851 for public executions.

"

J'aime Paris, but
I'm not really sure
Paris likes me.

"

Emily in Paris, 2020

Paris has its own Statue of Liberty.

New York's Lady Liberty was a gift from the French and they kept a small replica to symbolize the friendship between France and the USA.

"

In a nutshell (and, trust me, I know her well), I'd say the Parisienne is completely cuckoo!

"

How to Be a Parisian, 2014

Uritrottoirs – a combination of the French words for urinal and pavement – were first introduced in Paris in 2018. The device, which promises an eco-solution to public peeing, is essentially a box containing hay with an opening in the front and flowers displayed on top. The hay is then transformed into compost for use in parks and gardens.

66

To err is human.
To loaf is Parisian.

99

Victor Hugo

Following the Climate Energy Plan of Paris aimed at reducing 75 per cent of greenhouse gas emissions by 2050, the *2050 Paris Smart City* project by Vincent Callebaut Architectures is an amazing research and development initiative with high-rise green buildings scattered around the city, giving it a futuristic, forest-like twist.

Station F is the centre of French tech and the largest start-up hub in Europe. It's located in the 13th arrondissement, a famous regenerated industrial neighbourhood where the Bibliothèque Mittérand was built in 1996 as four high-rise towers which host 15 million books.

66

Whoever does not visit Paris regularly will never really be elegant.

99

Honoré de Balzac

Paris' first *Maison de Couture*, Charles Frederick Worth, was created in 1858. By 1910, there were already 300,000 couturiers in Paris!

Parisians' haute couture
invented the military
dress code of camouflage,
which roughly translates as
"make up for the stage".

"

Add two letters
to Paris, and
it's paradis(e).

"

Jules Renard

CHAPTER
FIVE

Métro, Boulot, Dodo

The saying goes that the life of a Parisian can be summarized in three words: *Métro, Boulot* (Work) and *Dodo* (Sleep). If you're not a Parisian, it would be a mistake to drive or take a taxi for a long-distance ride. The fastest way to get anywhere is by metro. Also, Parisians are notorious for their unruly driving and aggressive horn blasts.

Other alternatives are the *vélib* (public bike) and *trottinettes* (e-scooters), which are the new fashion and have been known to transform the city into a jungle. Try one down the Champs Elysées; you'll feel like the queen/ king of the world!

With around 400 stations, Paris's metro network holds hidden secrets. One of those is that at least 14 of them were either never used, abandoned or no longer in use.

The Porte des Lilas station is rented out as a film set.

More than 5 million people per day use the Métro. After Moscow, it's the busiest underground network in Europe.

The Regie Autonome
des Transports Parisiens
(RATP), which runs all public
transport in the French capital,
commissioned an opinion poll
to discover why Parisians
were using the Métro less.
A common reply was:
"Ça pue." (It stinks.)

"

Paris… is a world meant for the walker alone, for only the pace of strolling can take in all the rich (if muted) detail.

Edmund White, *The Flâneur*, 2001

Paris Point Zero marks the supposedly exact centre of the city. It is located just outside of Notre-Dame Cathedral in the public square, inlaid in the concrete.

All other locations are thought to be measured as a distance radiating from this point. This very heart of Paris is often treated as a wishing well.

"

A walk about Paris
will provide lessons in
history, beauty, and in
the point of Life.

"

Thomas Jefferson

Paris' infamous *risqué* street, rue Saint-Denis, was historically the street used by the kings of France to enter and exit the city!

The famous touring boats on the Seine, les Bateaux-Mouches, were originally steamboats built on Quai Mouche (Fly Wharf) in Lyon for the International Exhibition in 1867 in Paris.

In 1950, a famous linguist pointed out that there was a spelling mistake, as Mouche needed to have an 's' to mark the plural. As a response, the owner of the Bateaux-Mouche company created a publicity hoax to celebrate the memory of the creator of these boats, the so-called Jean-Sébastien Mouche. It was a huge success even though Mr Mouche had never existed!

In 1783, on 21 November, the first manned free flight by the Montgolfier brothers left Château de La Muette in the 16th arrondissement for the Butte aux Cailles in the 13th arrondissement, taking 25 minutes to cross a distance of 12km (7 miles).

The hot-air balloon tradition has been kept alive and well in Paris, where you can enjoy an ascent at Parc Citroën in the Ballon de Paris.

The current largest urban transport development plan is called Le Grand Paris. It consists of a suburbs-only Métro line under construction beyond the outskirts of the city; the extension of the 12-year-old beltway tram circuit; the recent elimination of concentric fee zones for public transportation; and the new Jean Nouvel-designed Paris Philharmonic, which is perched on the inside of the *Périph* (the ring-road around the city). Completion is scheduled for 2030.

Paris is one of the most walkable cities. To walk from the farthest northern point of the city (Porte de la Seine Saint-Denis) to the farthest southern point (Porte de Vanves) takes about 3 hours (10 kilometres) at an average pace, which is not so much for one of the best known capitals of the world.

If you're caught in between a public transport strike, you'll quickly learn how to get around by foot, or on the city's self-service bikes or scooters!

Top 10 walks for the Parisian flâneur

Belleville

Canal Saint-Martin, from the Parc des Buttes-Chaumont

La Promenade Plantée (La Coulée Verte)

Jardin des Plantes

Jardin des Tuileries

La Petite Ceinture

Luxembourg Gardens and Saint Germain, from rue de Seine to the Champ de Mars

Marais: from the North Marais to the historic 4th arrondissement

Flea and antique markets at Saint-Ouen

Palais-Royal

In the past, signs were hung on the façade of almost every house or shop. They indicated where someone lived, and assisted residents and visitors in finding their way around Paris before a precise system of street numbering was introduced in accordance with a decree of 1805.

Signs frequently represented the product made or sold by craftsmen: for example, a key represented a locksmith and a wheatsheaf signified a baker's shop.

Signs also depicted themes from history, religion, the animal kingdom (horses, lions and cockerels), or the plant world (grapes and pine cones).

Many roads still bear the name of a sign to this day, such as rue du Chat-qui-Pêche (Street of the Fishing Cat) and rue du Plat-d'Etain (Street of the Pewter Dish).

If you happen to arrive in Paris
on a Saturday in the autumn
or winter, you may encounter
public protests. Demonstrations
traditionally begin at Place de la
Nation, rue du Faubourg Saint-
Antoine, and end at Bastille,
Châtelet or République.

Student protest routes historically
revolve around the Sorbonne.
The famous riots of May 1968 took
place on rue Soufflot.

Sous les pavés, la Plage

(Under the cobblestones,
the beach)

Famous May 1968 slogan

By the 1850s there were approximately 150 covered passages in Paris, but this decreased greatly as a result of Haussmann's renovation of the city. These arcades covered with glass roofs, created by piercing through other buildings, are a typically Parisian architectural feature.

Most of them now house shops, tearooms and restaurants. There are around 20 of them in Paris in the vicinity of the Grands Boulevards.

In the late 18th century and the beginning of the 19th, covered passages were shortcuts between the busy, muddy streets of Paris where you could shop easily and at your leisure. Galerie Vivienne, at Palais Royal, quickly became one of the most iconic.

After a decline in the mid-1900s, they have since experienced a revival, with *haute couture* brands relocating their stores there.

"

The shopping, the food, the views! Paris is a city that entrances us all – and I'm no exception.

"

Michael Kors

Paris is the queen of micro-mobility in the city, with the *Vélib*, the self-service bicycle hire scheme, having started in 2007 with a fleet of 20,000 mechanical and electrical bikes.

The advent of the e-scooter era was in 2018, with a fleet of 15,000 provided by three private operators.

"

That Paris exists and anyone could choose to live anywhere else in the world will always be a mystery to me.

"

Midnight in Paris, 2011

The 10 most beautiful Métro stations

Louvre-Rivoli

Concorde

Varenne

Cluny-La Sorbonne

Pont Neuf

Palais Royal

Bastille

Arts et Métiers

Liège

Hôtel de Ville

Paris' green driving
goal is 2030.

By that date cars
using fossil fuels will be
entirely forbidden.

"

I totally agree that it makes sound ecological sense to use public transport. That said, here's one extremely good reason to take taxis: I always have the most surprising conversations with cab drivers. Well, perhaps not always. But over the years, I've had some pretty memorable ones!

"

Nicky Gentil, *Taxi Tales from Paris*, 2019

Place de l'Etoile, the roundabout circling the Arc the Triomphe, is the notoriously scary and jam-packed driving climax in Paris. The gigantic intersection has a diameter of 200 metres, with 12 avenues leading to it and no traffic lights!

It distributes traffic on perfect perspectives, from the Concorde to la Défense, and Saint-Augustin to the Trocadéro. If you're in a taxi, it is definitely one to avoid, but if it's dawn and Paris is calm as a desert, hop on one and enjoy the beautiful ride.

In 1914, taxis saved Paris from German invasion.

The German army were at 50km from Paris, and Galliéni, the head of the army, was missing 5,000 men to push them back east. Count Walewski, the clever owner of a Parisian taxi firm now called G7, requisitioned 1,500 of his taxis to take the *piou-pious* (foot-soldiers) to the enemy line. Paris was saved and the Germans had to retreat to the Aisne region where the Great War was to continue along the trenches. This resulted in a taxi invoice for the French government worth 70,000 francs!

CHAPTER

SIX

Secret Paris

Paris' intrigue lies behind its cobbled streets, covered passages and unknown paths.

If you step aside from the notorious landmarks, you might unravel some of the city's best-kept secrets – but you'll still be just scratching the surface!

66

Secrets travel fast in Paris.

99

Napoleon

Did you know that Egyptian mummies were mistakenly buried under the Bastille column? When bodies of the martyrs from the 1830 Revolution were relocated from their original graves, mummies which had also been stored at the same location following Napoleon's Egyptian campaign were part of the convoy. Who knows if their spirits managed to cross the Canal St Martin, which runs under the column!

From Bastille to the Mouzaïa district, eastern Paris is home to countless courtyards and passageways, away from the hustle and bustle of the city streets.

Historically, Faubourg Saint-Antoine was the hub of artisans, and passageways provided access to their workshops, away from dirty and muddy streets.

In the 19th arrondissement, the Mouzaïa area is a multitude of villas, cobbled streets with houses and flowery gardens.

It is also called *la Campagne* (the countryside), although it's not far from the heart of Paris. It is now also known for being the home of François Hollande.

Père Lachaise is Paris's most sought-after burial ground. Honoré de Balzac, Colette, Eugène Delacroix, Frédéric Chopin, Maria Callas and Sarah Bernhardt are just a few of the famous artists who made their final stop there. The VIP list includes 40 singers, 40 composers and 75 painters.

Jim Morrison's is the most visited tomb, with hoardes of fans coming to pay their respect on 3 July, the anniversary of his death.

Paris isn't a city,
it's a world.

King Francis I

La Goutte d'Or is the African corner of Paris. It bears the spirit of Dakar and Bamako!

Its centre, Boulevard Barbès, was named after Armand Barbès, a French politician born in Pointe-à-Pitre in Guadeloupe. He was an opponent to the July monarchy of 1848.

Up until the 18th century, wine of a golden colour was produced there, hence the name of the area, 'The Golden Drop'. Today the *Goutte d'or* company has switched to brewing beer.

So many films and TV series have been shot in the City of Light.

Gossip Girl will take you to the Marais district at bistro Chez Julien or café Louis-Philippe, then to the Galeries Lafayette and Printemps department stores for shopping, finishing at the Palais-Royal garden to eat a Pierre Hermé macaron.

Like Blair, have the best Paris fast food while walking on the Pont des Arts.

As for Blair and Serena's luxury walkabouts, 29 av de Montaigne is where you'll find the Harry Winston jewellery shop, and the Baccarat gallery museum is at 11 Place des Etats-Unis in the 16th arrondissement.

*Paris sera toujours Paris.
Qu'est-ce que tu veux qu'il
fasse d'autre?*

(Paris will always be Paris.
What else can Paris do?)

Frédéric Dard

The City of Love was a city of pleasures from the very beginning.

In the mid-19th century, a census counted 50,000 prostitutes in Paris. Toulouse Lautrec famously immortalised *les bordels* (house of pleasures) in his paintings.

The film *Moulin Rouge* illustrated the golden era of cabaret and courtisan world in the Pigalle district in Montmartre.

Top 10 alternative Paris attractions to visit

Ballroom dancing at the waterfront at the Jardin Tino Rossi

Musée du Quai Branly

The Archaeological Crypt near Notre-Dame reveals the centre of the old Roman city of Lutetia, right on the Île de la Cité

Stroll along the Promenade Plantée and Viaduc des Arts

Explore 19th-century covered passages: fewer than 30 of these ancestors of department stores still exist

Enjoy fine wine at the Canal St Martin, in the summer, sitting on the stony edge of the bank, with the rest of the Boho-Chic Parisian crowd

Appreciate Paris' street art at Canal St Martin in the 10th arrondissement

Make a visit to the trendy neighbourhood of Belleville

The Nuit Blanche festival, held every autumn: one night a year, art galleries and museums are open all night, for free

The Fête de la Musique: on the first day of the summer season, 21 June, music concerts are held all over the city for free in concert halls and outside in the streets

The true Parisian doesn't like Paris, but he cannot live elsewhere.

Alphonse Karr

Urinals in the shape of a giant mouth with red lipstick? Find this Rolling Stones reference in the hip bar called the Belushi in the 19th arrondissement.

Other memorable toilets hide in the Très Honoré bar, where twin thrones offer the perfect seat for an improvised chat.

Roland Garros, otherwise known as the French Open, was first played in 1891 on sand. For the first six years it was only open to men; women weren't allowed to take part until 1897.

The clay surface isn't actually clay – 44,000kg of crushed red brick are used each year to give it its unique orange colour.

The PSG Stadium is called Le Parc des Princes (The Princes' Park). The club's colours are red, white and blue with the symbol of the Eiffel Tower.

Red and blue are Parisian colours (a nod to revolutionary figures such as La Fayette) and white is the symbol of royalty and Saint-Germain-en-Laye.

The quintessential *titi parisien* is Victor Hugo's Gavroche. According to the TFL dictionary, *le titi parisien* refers to the typical "parisian child" of the mid- to late 19th century. *Poulbot* means the same but the term is strictly reserved for Montmartre kids!

"

To be Parisian is not to be
born in Paris.
It's to be born again there.

"

Sacha Guitry

Since 1978, *The Rocky Horror Picture Show* has been showing at the Studio Galande cinema in the 5th arrondissement.

The tradition is that actors re-enact the movie scenes live on stage. After each gong, everyone chimes in "Master, dinner is prepared!"

The Cimetière des Chiens et Autres Animaux Domestiques is often claimed to be the first zoological necropolis in the modern world.

It opened in 1899 at 4 pont de Clichy on Île des Ravageurs in Asnières-sur-Seine (Greater Paris). *My kingdom for a dog!*

Every summer a secret location is allocated for the *Dîner en blanc.*

In the month of June, 10,000 people attend a chic pop-up white-tablecloth dinner out in the open in the City of Love.

Dress code: white, *obviously.*

Paris! Paris outragé! Paris brisé! Paris martyrisé! Mais Paris, libéré!

(Paris! Paris outraged! Paris broken! Paris tortured! But Paris, free again!)

Charles de Gaulle

La Verticale de la Tour Eiffel is the annual race up the Iron Lady's stairs.

The winner is the one who manages to reach the entrance of the staircase first and run up the 1,665 steps, with an elevation gain of 279 metres.

Once a month, the hairdresser Djelani Maachi offers to cut hair during a full moon, on the place des Victoires, by the statue of Louis XV.

Moonlight will apparently help your hair grow stronger and healthier!

Heart-stopping news!

It was common in the 17th and 18th arrondissements to embalm the hearts of kings, queens, princes and princesses.

The Val de Grâce Chapel in the 5th arrondissement was at one time the home of 50 royal hearts!

These organs were highly coveted
by painters, who extracted from
them a particular substance which,
when mixed with oil, formed a
very unique texture and colour.
Because of this, the revolutionary
"sans-culottes" sold the precious
hearts for paintings that would later
be exhibited at the Louvre,
such as *Intérieur d'une Cuisine* by
Michel Martin Drolling.

In the 1980s, artists made their creative home in the old refrigerating warehouses of Paris, called Les Frigos. Its space is open to the public, with 120 artists working on site and 80 workshops in total. Just remember to pack a sweater or two!

Les Frigos is located in the 13th arrondissement, the ex-industrial area of Paris, which has now become the hub of new architecture, culture and tech.

Get free accommodation and become a millionaire in Paris, on one condition. You will have to take up the challenge of living in the Père Lachaise tomb of the Russian countess Elisabeth Demidoff, who died in 1818.

You will be allowed to go outside to exercise only at night when the cemetery is closed, and have meals delivered to your door. If you manage to tolerate such a life (or death; depends how you see it!) for a whole year, you'll be entitled to the countess' fortune, bequeathed in this strangest of wills.

"

Everything starts in Paris.

"

Nancy Spain